TABLES PRACTICE 2

Games and puzzles to practise the 6, 7, 8 and 9 times tables

Richard Dawson

MACMILLAN
CHILDREN'S BOOKS

Can you remember your 2× table?
Cut out the flowers and stick them on the correct stalks, then colour the plants.

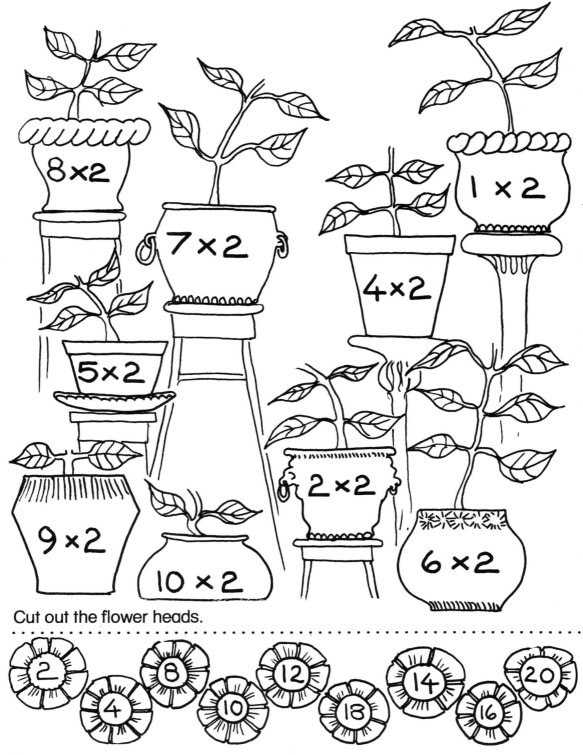

Cut out the flower heads.

Can you help the frog round the pond? Colour the leaves of the 5× table to find his route.

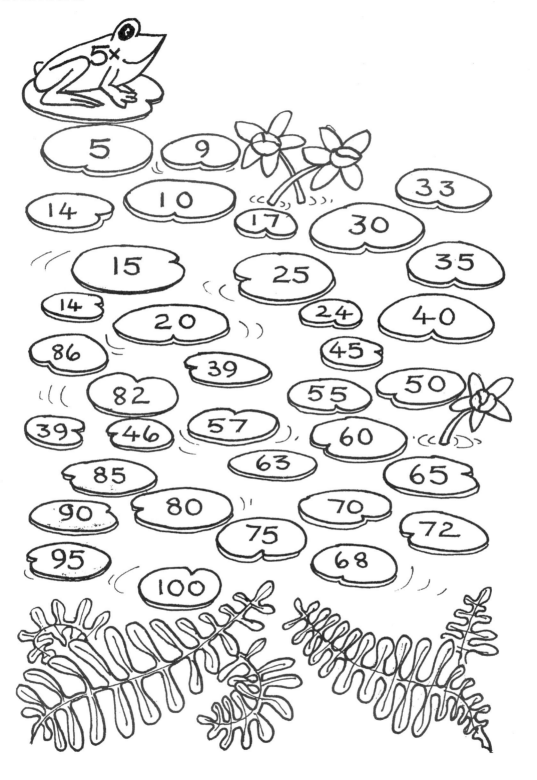

Put each jockey on the correct horse.

Cut out the jockeys.

Use the 3× table to find each person's hat, then draw it on the correct head.

Can you remember your 10× table?
Join the dots then colour the picture.

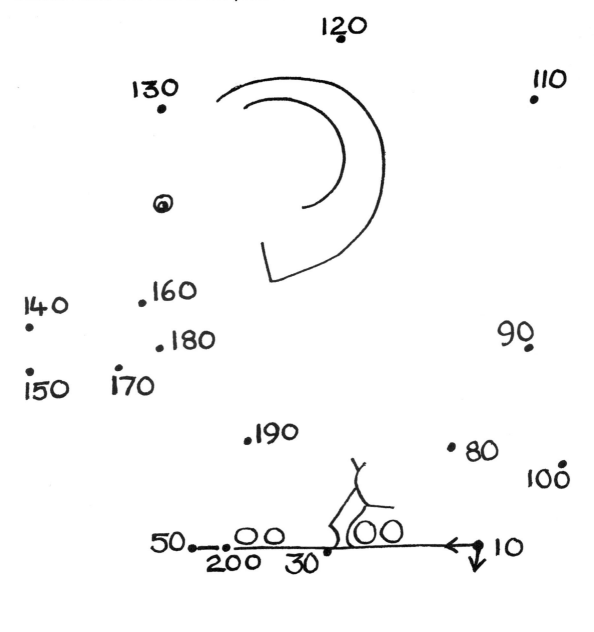

Use the 6× table to join each caterpillar to its butterfly, then colour the butterflies.

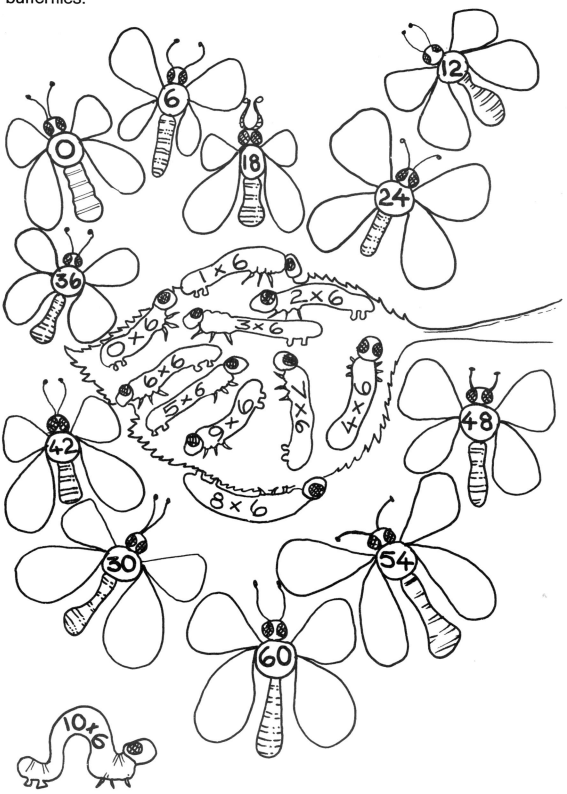

Ring sets of ladybirds to make the number of spots answer the sums. Write the number of spots in each set.

1 × 6

2 × 6

3 × 6

4 × 6

5 × 6

6 × 6

8 × 6

9 × 6

7 × 6

10 × 6

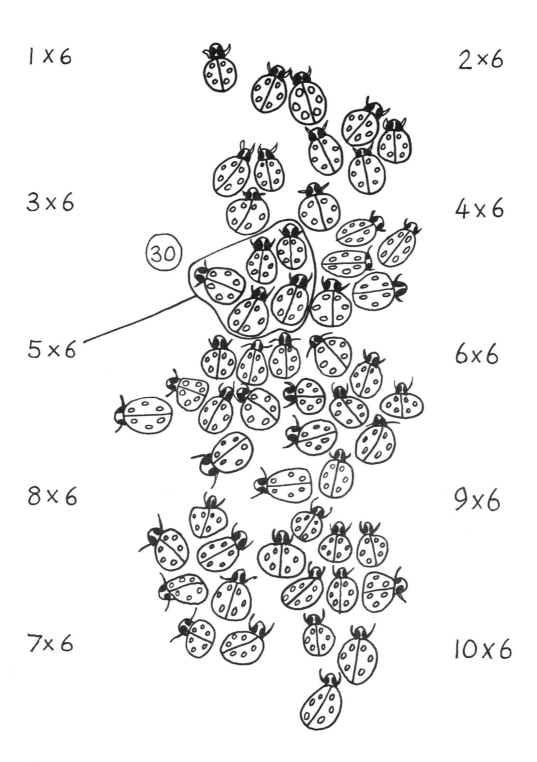

8

Use your ruler to join the sums to their answers.
What have you drawn? _____

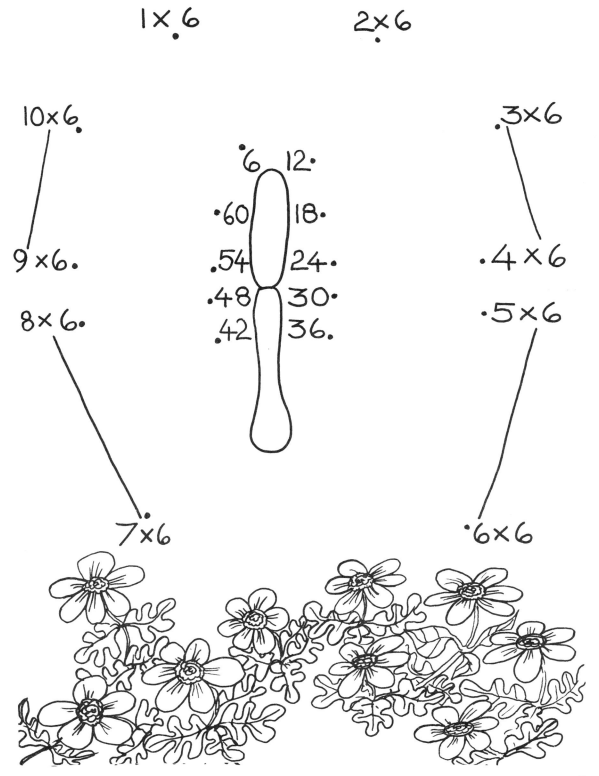

Cut out the flies and stick them on the web on the correct spot.

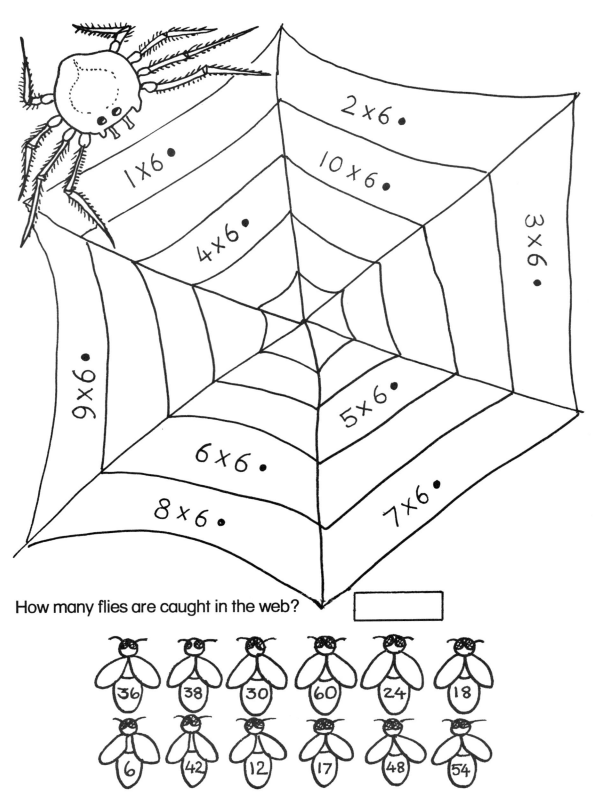

How many flies are caught in the web?

Answer the sums in the beehives . . .

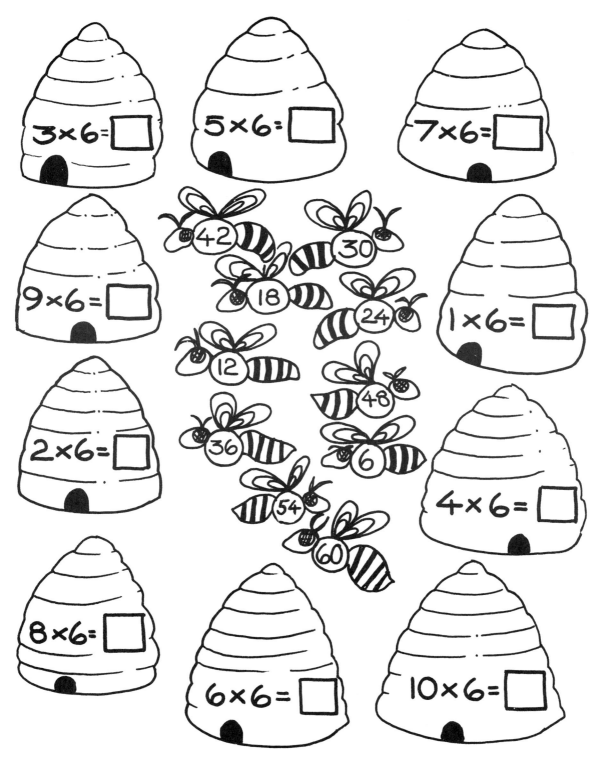

. . . now join the bees to their own hives.

Can you shoot the apples off the heads? Use a ruler to draw the line.

First do the sums. Use the answers to join the dots and complete the picture.

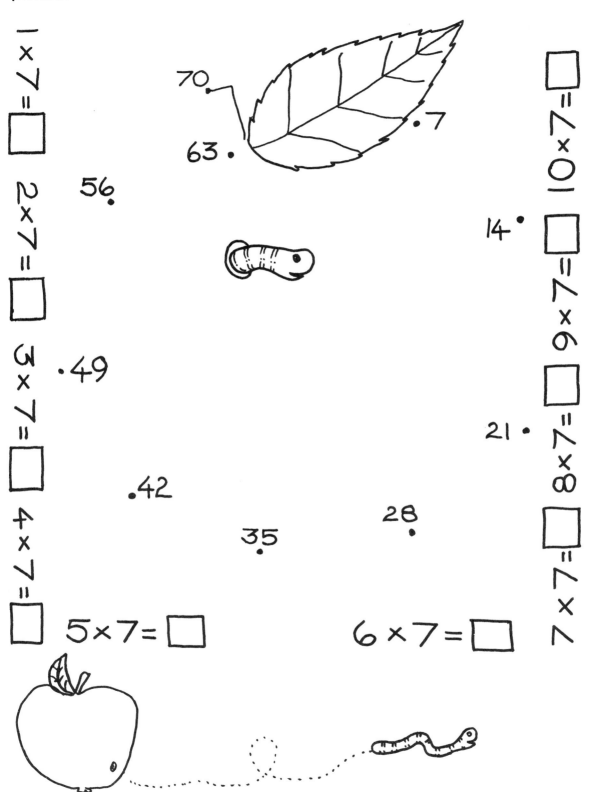

$1 \times 7 = \square$
$2 \times 7 = \square$
$3 \times 7 = \square$
$4 \times 7 = \square$
$5 \times 7 = \square$
$6 \times 7 = \square$
$7 \times 7 = \square$
$8 \times 7 = \square$
$9 \times 7 = \square$
$10 \times 7 = \square$

Copy the correct apples onto the shelves to complete the 7× table sums.

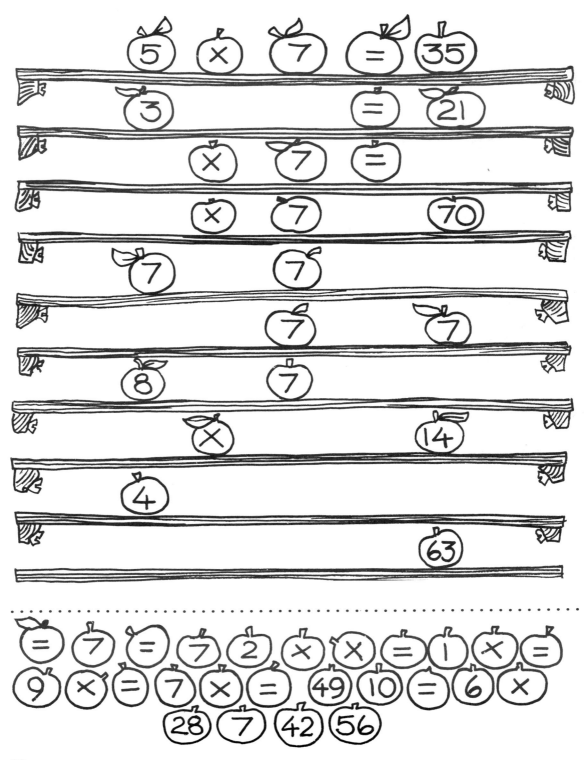

Use the 7× table to join each worm to its own apple.

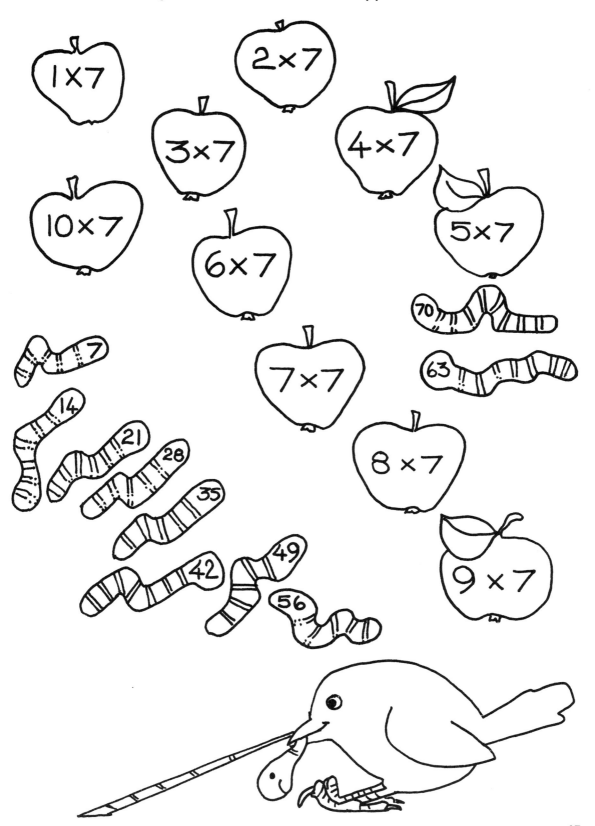

Carefully cut out each mouse and stick it on top of its cheese.

Use the 7x table to join the cats to the mice they will catch.
Not all the cats are awake!

Make it snappy! Answer the sums as quickly as you can.

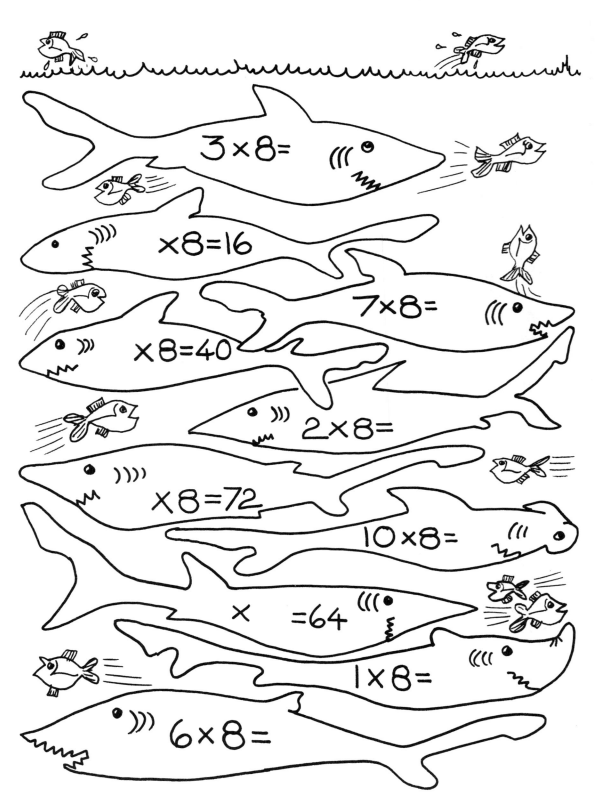

Colour all the 8× table crabs the same colour.

Use the 8× table to join the dots.

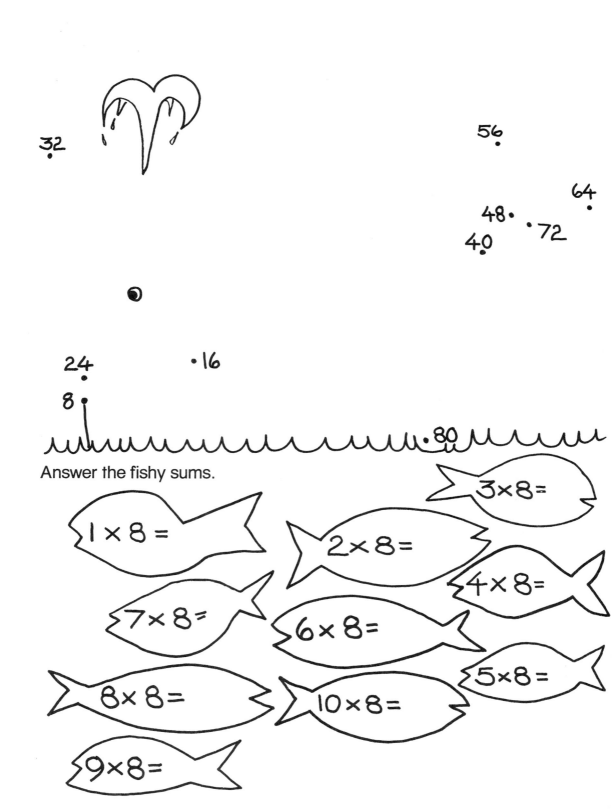

Answer the fishy sums.

1 × 8 =
3 × 8 =
2 × 8 =
4 × 8 =
7 × 8 =
6 × 8 =
5 × 8 =
8 × 8 =
10 × 8 =
9 × 8 =

Answer the times tables to fill in each turtle shell.

Guidelines: This page is a review of the 6, 7 and 8× tables. If the child has difficulty with the answers, it would be advisable to go through the practice pages of each table again.

Hold your breath whilst you answer the sums!
Try to say all the sums aloud in one breath.

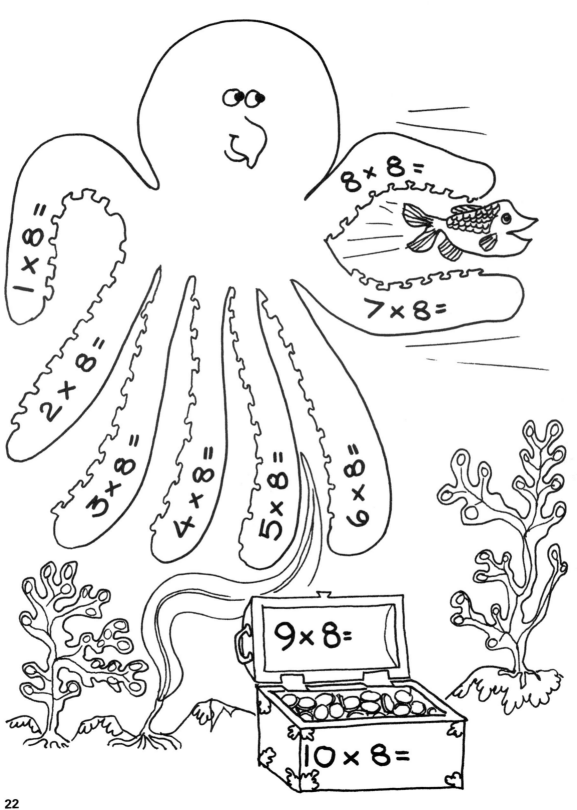

Can you use the 8× table to sail the ship from island to island?

Cut out the parachutists and stick them on the correct parachute.

Colour the winning 9× table team red and plot the ball's route to the goal.

Fill in all the missing numbers, then do the sums round the edge.

1 × 9 =

18 = 9 ×

3 × 9 =

36 = 4 ×

5 × 9 =

= 6 × 9

× = 63

= 8 × 9

× = 81

= 10 × 9

1 × 9 = ☐

2 × 9 = ☐

3 × 9 = ☐

4 × 9 = ☐

6 × 9 = ☐

7 × 9 = ☐

8 × 9 = ☐

9 × 9 = ☐

5 × 9 = ☐

10 × 9 = ☐

Colour all the 6× snails' heads red.
Colour all the 8× snails' shells blue.
Colour all the 9× snails' tails green.

Which snails are more than one colour?

How quickly can you lap the track by answering the sums?

Can you answer the sums and then plot the horse's route around the course?

Fill in the tables square.
You'll find it a real treasure map in the future.

Here are the 2, 3, 4, 5, 6, 7, 8, 9 and 10 times tables in full in case you need them. It's useful to learn them by heart.

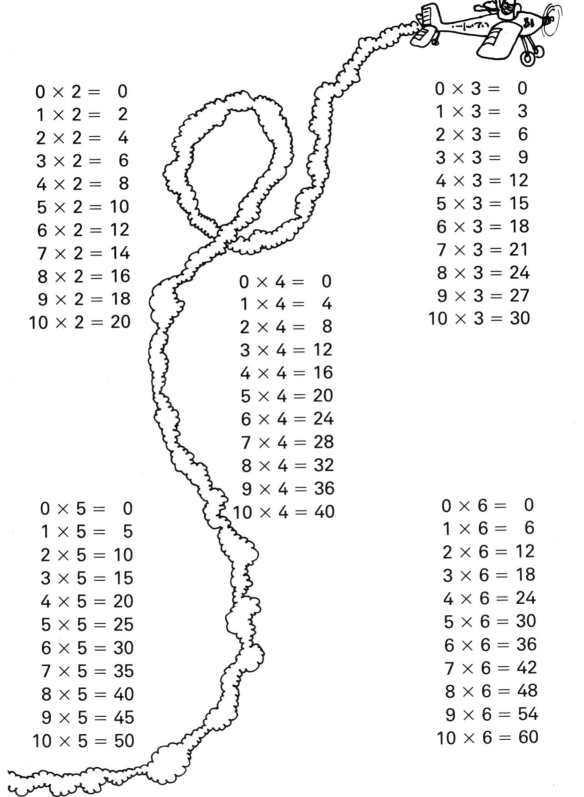

0 × 2 = 0		0 × 3 = 0
1 × 2 = 2		1 × 3 = 3
2 × 2 = 4		2 × 3 = 6
3 × 2 = 6		3 × 3 = 9
4 × 2 = 8		4 × 3 = 12
5 × 2 = 10		5 × 3 = 15
6 × 2 = 12		6 × 3 = 18
7 × 2 = 14		7 × 3 = 21
8 × 2 = 16	0 × 4 = 0	8 × 3 = 24
9 × 2 = 18	1 × 4 = 4	9 × 3 = 27
10 × 2 = 20	2 × 4 = 8	10 × 3 = 30
	3 × 4 = 12	
	4 × 4 = 16	
	5 × 4 = 20	
	6 × 4 = 24	
	7 × 4 = 28	
	8 × 4 = 32	
	9 × 4 = 36	
0 × 5 = 0	10 × 4 = 40	0 × 6 = 0
1 × 5 = 5		1 × 6 = 6
2 × 5 = 10		2 × 6 = 12
3 × 5 = 15		3 × 6 = 18
4 × 5 = 20		4 × 6 = 24
5 × 5 = 25		5 × 6 = 30
6 × 5 = 30		6 × 6 = 36
7 × 5 = 35		7 × 6 = 42
8 × 5 = 40		8 × 6 = 48
9 × 5 = 45		9 × 6 = 54
10 × 5 = 50		10 × 6 = 60

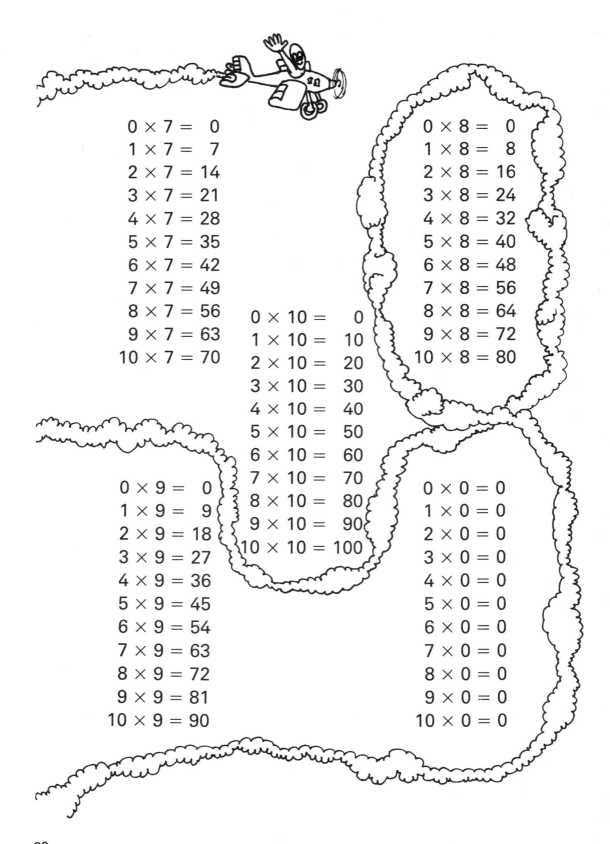

0 × 7 = 0	0 × 8 = 0	
1 × 7 = 7	1 × 8 = 8	
2 × 7 = 14	2 × 8 = 16	
3 × 7 = 21	3 × 8 = 24	
4 × 7 = 28	4 × 8 = 32	
5 × 7 = 35	5 × 8 = 40	
6 × 7 = 42	6 × 8 = 48	
7 × 7 = 49	7 × 8 = 56	
8 × 7 = 56	8 × 8 = 64	
9 × 7 = 63	9 × 8 = 72	
10 × 7 = 70	10 × 8 = 80	

| 0 × 10 = 0 |
| 1 × 10 = 10 |
| 2 × 10 = 20 |
| 3 × 10 = 30 |
| 4 × 10 = 40 |
| 5 × 10 = 50 |
| 6 × 10 = 60 |
| 7 × 10 = 70 |
| 8 × 10 = 80 |
| 9 × 10 = 90 |
| 10 × 10 = 100 |

0 × 9 = 0	0 × 0 = 0
1 × 9 = 9	1 × 0 = 0
2 × 9 = 18	2 × 0 = 0
3 × 9 = 27	3 × 0 = 0
4 × 9 = 36	4 × 0 = 0
5 × 9 = 45	5 × 0 = 0
6 × 9 = 54	6 × 0 = 0
7 × 9 = 63	7 × 0 = 0
8 × 9 = 72	8 × 0 = 0
9 × 9 = 81	9 × 0 = 0
10 × 9 = 90	10 × 0 = 0